Nature Explorers

Backyards and Parks

Nick Baker

Collins
An Imprint of HarperCollinsPublishers

For my niece Rowan and the many adventures we are yet to have.

ISBN: 978-0-00-720766-4
ISBN-10: 0-00-720766-2

www.harpercollins.com

ISBN: 978-0-06-089079-7 (in the United States)
ISBN-10: 0-06-089079-7

FIRST U.S. EDITION Published in 2007.
HarperCollins books may be purchased
for educational, business, or sales promotional use. For
information in the United States, please write to:
Special Markets Department, HarperCollins Publishers,
10 East 53rd Street, New York, NY 10022.

The name of the "Smithsonian," "Smithsonian
Institution," and the sunburst logo are registered
trademarks of the Smithsonian Institution.

Text © Nick Baker 2007
Photographer: Nikki English, except for those pictures credited on page 71
Flick book illustrations: Lizzie Harper
Colour reproduction by Dot Gradations Ltd, UK
Printed and bound by Printing Express, Hong Kong

10 09 08 07
7 6 5 4 3 2 1

Disclaimer: Many of the projects in this book involve tools, knives, fire, or cooking. All of these can be
dangerous and require a good deal of training and practice before they are safely used. Parents should
supervise these activities and monitor the correct use of tools until children can be considered
competent to use them themselves. In addition, common sense and basic precautions—knowing
exactly where your children are and what they are doing at all times, making sure they wear
sunscreen and appropriate, protective clothing, and teaching them how to respect nature and safely
explore their surroundings—are the key to your children learning the joys of the great outdoors.

Contents

Flick the pages to see the bird fly!

Your local patch

There is no place like home. You may not think of looking for adventure among the patio tubs, behind the woodpile, or even in the potting shed or window box, but it is there in abundance. The trick is to change your perspective on life, look at things from a different place and in a new way.

 You may feel there is no interesting wildlife for hundreds of miles, but change your scale a bit and you can be running with predators every bit as ferocious as a lion or tiger. You can stalk creatures as exotic and alien in their appearance as any bird of paradise and witness phenomena that would boggle the mind of even the most world-weary scientist—all within a few yards of where you are sitting right now!

You don't believe me? Get out there and look. This book is about giving you wings to explore this seemingly familiar environment. Within these pages I give away little tips and tricks that make the natural world reveal itself in amazing ways. The pages are peppered with suggestions of things to look out for and—of course— some of the easier ways to interact with wildlife and make your own patch more attractive to the small creatures that live in your garden, window box, or patio.

The basic requirements of life include somewhere to live and preferably with the other essentials to fuel and nourish: namely food and water. Even if you live somewhere that seems like a concrete desert, get down and look into the cracks and crevices and here you will find all the essentials for life. You just might be surprised as to what is living close to your own home. Look at a crack in a patio; this is shelter for something very small as, in here, there will be moisture and warmth.

You can also create homes and provide food and water to boost the number of species sharing your space; these ideas and more are explored within the pages of this book. Remember, though, this is not a comprehensive guide, so have fun, experiment, and think about other ways you can encourage and study the wildlife around you.

Home Sweet Home—you may be lucky enough to have barn swallows nesting under your eaves.

All flowers lure insects; from bees and hoverflies to butterflies, they all add interest to your garden.

Where you have flying insects, you will also start attracting those that feed on them—birds, bats, and, of course, spiders.

Handy stuff for exploring

What tools you will need to explore your backyard or park with very much depends on what your area is like. If you have a little backyard in the city with hardly enough space to swing a net, you will explore it differently than someone who has a mountain in theirs. Having said this, there is interest to be found in any garden from an estate to a window box, and so here are a few items that I would find useful when exploring.

Binoculars These are always very useful, especially if you want to watch the details of the lives of birds and other insects without disturbing them. A pair of binoculars may be quite expensive to buy, but they are invaluable to a serious naturalist.

First aid kit Keep a fully equipped kit close by at all times, including insect repellent, sunscreen, antiseptic spray, and band aids.

Magnifying glass/pocket microscope Most things you can make or improvize, but a hand lens is an essential piece of equipment. It needn't be expensive and you can pick one up for pocket money. If you want to turn mosquitoes into monsters, though, you may need a pocket microscope. This is a bit more expensive, but worth every penny and still a fraction of the price of a Playstation!

Notebook and pen/pencil More naturalist's staples, it's always good to make notes, keep diaries, and draw the things you notice. It is something all the great naturalists from Darwin to Bill Oddie have done. It is surprising just how quickly we forget details.

Plastic pots and jars These are staples of any naturalist anywhere; handy for storing specimens, rearing insects, or simply holding onto something while you inspect it with a magnifying glass. Plastic bags can do a similar job and you can keep a handful in your pocket at any time. They are useful for storing botanical plants and, if you blow them up and tie the tops with string, you can make temporary containers from them.

Sieves You may be surprised, but meshed scooping devices from sieves to tea strainers can make very handy little catching devices! They can be used like a net in water or modified into a pair of bug-catching tongs. Use larger sieves to sift through soil to find small creatures and moth pupae.

Trowel I find this handy for investigating the soil, digging up worms and, of course, for repairing any footprints you might leave on your parents' flower beds. It's always a good idea not to upset those garden proud grown-ups.

Plastic boxes

Glass jar

Microscope

Test tubes

Small sieve

Magnifying glass

Magnifying lens

Notebook and pen

Plastic bags

Binoculars

Trowel

Take my advice

* Because this book is about attracting things to your garden and providing homes and feeding stations, there is obviously plenty of creating to be done. This means there are sections and activities that involve hammers, nails, screws, and even the odd drill and other power tools. These things can be a little tricky to use and can be dangerous.

* So before you start any of the projects, let a grown-up know what you are up to and, if you are using specialist tools, ask for help.

Our feathered friends

Birds are everywhere, and because they are big, they are often the first creatures to catch our attention. They also show us how we can provide for nature in our own backyards. In fact, if it wasn't for our feathered friends, we wouldn't be seeing our gardens and parks as wildlife refuges at all. Birds invented wildlife-friendly gardening!

In recent years, watching birds in backyards and being aware of who visits and in what numbers has given us a better understanding of just how bird populations are changing. It also shows how important the wildlife garden can be in supporting many species.

There are many products, catalogs, and shops dedicated to encouraging birds into your garden, and once you have gained their interest, the feeling of successfully helping them makes your heart glow. So why stop at birds, why not encourage butterflies and other insects, mammals, and reptiles and amphibians, also?

There is more to encouraging birds into your garden than hanging out a bag of seeds or throwing out some stale bread when the generous mood takes you! Birds are feathered ambassadors for what we humans can do for wildlife. Just by nailing together a few planks of wood and providing a variety of food and a source of water, we can make their lives easier. They will return the favor by giving us a little glimpse into their often fascinating lives.

Bird populations in the wild depend mainly on two things: first they need food, and second they need somewhere to live and nest. So if you are to make your local patch of interest to our feathered friends you need to bear these things in mind.

American goldfinches are fond of eating thistle seed and line their nests with thistle down late in the summer.

Barn swallows love to nest on our homes and outbuildings. It's hard to imagine that they come all the way from South America every summer just to stick mud together under our eaves!

Male cardinals are bright spots in many suburban backyards. They start singing earlier in the spring than many of our songbirds.

Wrens are the kings of the singers; small birds with loud voices that love a garden with untidy corners and dense shrubs.

It's a two-way relationship

Feeding the birds is probably the single most popular way in which people interact with the natural world, from feeding pigeons on the park bench to the bird table in the backyard. What you are doing is simply taking on the needs and requirements of the birds.

The ways you can present food to birds is becoming big business, and by using the right mix of foods and the right feeder in the right place, you can attract birds easily. But for now, here's an inexpensive idea to get you started (see opposite).

Niger seed

White praso millet

Raisins

Oatmeal

Black oil sunflower seeds

Hemp seed

Peanut hearts

Cut corn

Canary seed

High-energy treat

Sunflower seeds

Choose a variety of foods. Not all birds like eating the same things—finches love seeds (niger and sunflower), titmice are crazy about peanut butter, orioles like fruit, and woodpeckers love fatty, suet-based stuff

YOU WILL NEED

> **1 quart plastic milk carton**
> **marker pen**
> **ruler**
> **scissors**
> **twigs**
> **bird seed**
> **funnel**
> **string**

1 Using the marker pen and ruler, draw a line ¾ inch from the bottom of the plastic milk carton and parallel to the base on the opposite side to the handle.

2 With the scissors, cut along the marked line and then, at each end of the incision, cut up about 1¼ inches.

3 Fold the flap you have just created back into the bottle and add a perch or two. Make these from twigs or any straight bits of wood; push them into a hole below the feeding tray.

4 Fill with seeds, pouring them into the container through a funnel. Screw the lid back on and then hang up the container with string in your backyard.

Take my advice

* Position your feeders carefully. Birds like to be in the open so that predators cannot sneak up on them. But they also like to have cover nearby so that if a sharp-shinned hawk comes cruising around, they can all leap into cover.

* Vary the locations of your feeders, as some birds are bold while others are shy. So feed close to the house by all means, but do not forget the nervous ones and provide food at the end of the garden as well.

* Different birds feed in different ways. Some rarely get onto the bird table but prefer to stay on the ground, while others like flat surfaces, and some like to hang.

* Feed only good quality foods. If it's cheap, it may have lots of wheat in it. Cheaper peanuts may also contain a fungus infection that can kill the birds you are trying to help.

Nut feeders

The cheapest nut feeder has to be a plastic mesh bag, the sort that supermarket fruit often comes in. Simply stuff it with peanuts and hang it up. I hate the bright orange of the netting but I have noticed that siskins (one of my favorite birds) show the most interest in these feeders even though they have many others (some of them very expensive, also) to choose from. This could well become a subject for a garden experiment!

Alternatively, make a full-fat pudding. This animal fat-based food is made from warmed animal fat or suet, mixed with any variety of seeds, fruits, nuts, or insects and left to set before being served up. It's a great way of providing a high-energy winter diet for your birds. My favorite way to use the suet recipe is to make fat cones—see opposite—or dip teasel heads into the melted suet.

Another way to provide a suet cake is to leave the mix to set in a tin that is wedged in place between three blocks screwed to your bird table. Or you can form a ball and stuff it in a plastic fruit net; fill an old coconut shell; or drill holes in a log and jam the fat into these. This last is a real favorite for woodpeckers! This recipe is very easy to make and you can fine tune the ingredients, perhaps including some thistle seed, sunflower seeds, or millet, according to what the birds seem to prefer.

Take my advice

* If you have just started feeding the birds in your garden, it may take them a little while to learn about your new service. So be patient and if after a few weeks there are still no visitors, try relocating your feeding station. It may be that the birds feel just a little too exposed.

* Keep your feeders clean by washing and sterilizing them every few months and try to avoid food hanging around and becoming stale. Feeders over concrete or decking mean you can easily sweep away any spilled food, which may otherwise attract unwanted wildlife such as rats.

1 Next time you are out for a walk collect old dry pine cones in various sizes. When you get home, tie some string around the base of a few of them.

2 Take a saucepan and heat the shortening slowly in it until it has melted. Add the peanut butter and mix in until it has melted as well.

3 Add some flour to help thicken the mixture and then pour in plenty of small fine seeds until you have a fairly stiff mixture. Let it cool a little, continuing to stir.

4 Before the mixture sets, drop your cones into the pan and press the concoction in between the scales.

5 Leave to cool and harden and then take out to the garden to hang in a tree or on a bird table.

Hummingbird hospitality

Hummingbirds are among the most amazing and beautiful birds on earth. One species—the Bee Hummingbird of Cuba—is the world's smallest bird at 2½ inches, while the Giant Hummingbird of South America is the size of a robin! The 320 species hummingbirds live only in the Americas, and 15 of these nest in the United States and Canada.

If you would like to attract hummingbirds to your garden but don't have the right plants to feed them naturally, you could make an artificial feeder from a few simple household items. You will need: a small, clear (untinted) bottle such as a vanilla bottle or aspirin vial; pipe cleaners or wire; red yarn, ribbon, or tape. To make the feeder, just follow these three simple steps: 1. Remove the cap from a small mouthed-bottle and wind a pipe cleaner or other wire tightly around the neck, leaving enough to wrap the other end around a tree branch.

(continued opposite)

Take my advice

* Of course hummingbirds don't need artificial feeders, and another way to attract them is to plant a garden filled with their favorite flowers. They visit many different flowers, but bee-balm, Impatiens, honeysuckle, Nicotiana, and phlox are among their favorites. Plant species that will bloom throughout hummingbird season (May–September in the North) and make big patches of color (remember red is their favorite color, followed by yellow). A flower bed will also attract insects—which make up about 50% of a hummingbird's diet. If you make your yard attractive enough, the hummingbirds will come.

Nick's trick

If you manage to make an artificial feeder for hummingbirds, make your feeder look like a big flower by tying a bright red bow around it or wrapping it in red tape (hummingbirds like red best).

The bodies of hummingbirds and the way they behave are unique in many ways. They can flap their wings as fast as 80 beats per second—that's what makes them hum! They can hover in one place while they sip nectar from flowers and even fly backwards. When they feed, it looks like they use their long bills like a soda straw, but actually, they sort of pump the nectar in along a groove in the tongue.

The bright iridescent color on a male hummingbird's throat (called a "gorget") is not a pigment like paint, but is a kind of optical illusion cause by microscopic parts of the feathers that reflect only certain parts of the light spectrum—think crystals or rainbows. This flashy neckwear helps attract females and the first time you see it flash in the sun, you probably won't believe your eyes.

Despite their small size, hummingbirds are not at all shy. In fact they can be quite aggressive. With a few simple items, you may be able to attract them to your yard.

2. Mix a nectar solution of 1 part sugar to 4 parts water and fill the bottle. After it's mixed, boil it for 10 minutes to sterilize it.
3. Fill the bottle to the brim with your nectar mix and hang your feeder from the branch of a tree where you can see it easily from your house. Have patience. It usually takes a while for hummingbirds to find a feeder.

Take it further

If hummingbirds visit your feeder in the summer they are probably nesting nearby. If you watch their behavior carefully and follow them for a while you may be able to find their nest. A hummingbird's nest is an incredible little cup made of lichen flakes bound together with spider webs and fixed to a tree branch. It really is a remarkable little construction and one of the wonders of the North American backyard. Watch the nest carefully and you will soon see two tiny bills poking up waiting to be fed. Then, keep a close eye on your hummingbirds' nest as their young ones grow.

Making a simple bird feeder

Go to any garden center and take a look at the bird feeders that are available.
You can get them with balconies, balustrades, porches, even thatched roofs and chimneys. Some even come with a nest box upstairs! Personally, I think that some of them are just too ornate. In my experience, although they can all work to a greater or lesser degree, they fall short of actually providing what the birds want and need, which is a nice stable, spacious platform that is easy to keep clean.

Birds will eat off pretty much anything and, as with all things to do with wildlife, there are no hard and fast rules, so you can experiment. To get you started, here is a very simple and effective step-by-step project to build a bird feeder.

1

The piece of plywood is the feeding platform and to this you need to attach the edging strips, two of which are a little shorter than the shorter sides of the plywood to give you gaps in the corners for making it easier to sweep clean. They also allow rainwater to drain off.

2

Screw the edging strips to the board. Use at least two screws on each short strip and three on the longer edges. At this stage, you can paint and protect the bird table with a water-based preservative, which will keep the wood from rotting.

3

Now attach your table to the post using the angle brackets, screwing the brackets to the post first.

4

Screw the brackets to the bottom of the feeding platform. You could also attach some hooks to the post and to the corners on the underside of the table to hang seed feeders and suet cakes from. Choose the location for your bird feeder and drive your post into the ground as far as it will go, with a minimum of 16 inches under the ground's surface. You can now coat this with wood preservative also.

YOU WILL NEED

> **15 x 20 inch piece of marine or exterior quality plywood, a minimum of ½ inch thick**
> **50 x ½ x ½ inch batten cut into two 10 inch lengths and two 16 inch lengths**
> **¾ inch galvanized wood screws**
> **Cross-head screwdriver**
> **Water-based wood preservative and paintbrush (optional)**
> **4 cup hooks**
> **6 foot wooden post with a flat top and a sharp end**
> **4 angle brackets**

Make a deluxe bird bath

It's good to provide water for your birds near the feeders. Let's face it, would you want to eat buckets full of cereal or chips without a drink to wash it all down? Birds will not only want to drink regularly but they also need to wash and keep their feathers clean.

The best way of providing water is an old tray, dish, or dustbin lid filled with water. Pop a rock or a branch in it so your visitors have somewhere to perch. In the winter it is even more vital to provide water, but you must make sure the water doesn't freeze over. Break up any ice that forms as soon as possible. Alternatively, make this handsome bird bath with just a few ingredients.

When you first turn over your bird bath there may be bits of cabbage stuck in it. Either cut them out with scissors or let nature take its course and they will soon shrivel up and die.

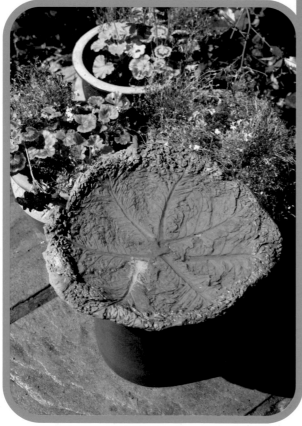

YOU WILL NEED

> a board
> 10 lb bag grit sand
> big cabbage
> 10 lb bag ready-mix cement
> water
> an old bucket
> stick
> rubber gloves
> polythylene sheet (or plastic bag)

1 First tip out the sand onto the board and make a mound out of it. The mound represents the depth and the size of your bird bath, so use your imagination.

2 Now cut the leaves off your cabbage, keeping them whole. Place them over the sand mound with their stems meeting in the middle.

3 Empty the bag of cement into the bucket and add water according to the instructions on the bag. Stir it thoroughly with a strong stick.

4 Pour the cement mix onto the top of the cabbage leaves and then, wearing the rubber gloves, spread it over the mound to a depth of at least 1 inch.

5 Make sure the cabbage leaves, and any sand that is showing through the leaves, are well covered with the cement. Then smooth the top of the cement to a round or flat shape, depending on what you're going to stand the bird bath on when it's finished.

6 Cover the whole thing with polythylene and leave to dry for at least a day. When the cement is dry, turn over the bath, remove the board, scoop out the sand, remove the leaves and you have it—a designer, custom-made bird bath with a beautiful, yet non-slip, leafy design in the bottom of it. You can varnish or paint it if you wish and then keep it filled with fresh clean water for happy splashy birds.

Make a birdhouse

Birds are experiencing a housing crisis and the reason there are not enough nest sites is—you've guessed it—us humans. We have a tendency to tidy up the countryside and our backyards too much. All too often, dead trees that offer all sorts of habitats, crevices, and holes are seen as a public safety hazard and so are cut down, just to be on the safe side. Even healthy trees are axed because a knot hole may get infected and kill the tree.

As a result of our human paranoia, the traditional nesting site for many of our small woodland birds—the hole—is sadly becoming a rare thing. So here is yet another way we can provide for our birds and at the same time learn an awful lot about their private lives; it comes in the form of a wren box.

This classic design—a wooden box with a hole in it—is the basis of many other boxes that cater for the needs and requirements of other species. Here I show you how to make the basic design, and if you get adventurous, overleaf are a few simple modifications and other ideas.

Making this birdhouse does require a little bit of woodwork. Now, I am useless with my hands but even I can make a half decent wren box that no self-respecting wren would turn its beak up at. So try it. Let's face it, a birdhouse is one woodwork lesson with an end product that will not be gathering dust on top of the wardrobe.

Cutting plan for your wood

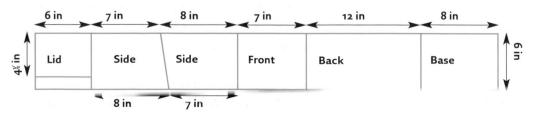

Lid	Side	Side	Front	Back	Base
6 in	7 in	8 in	7 in	12 in	8 in

4½ in   8 in   7 in   6 in

1 Ask an adult to help you cut up the wood as shown in the plan opposite. Use a special 2 inch plug cutter fitting on the electric drill to make the hole in the front. With a wooden drill bit, also make holes in the base for drainage. Then lay out the pieces as shown in this picture.

2 Using the cross-head screwdriver, screw the sides to the base, at the top, and bottom.

3 Screw the front to the sides and base. Again, use a screw at the top and bottom of each edge. Do the same with the back, ensuring the extra length is sticking out the top of the box, rather than the bottom.

4 The only piece you do not nail down is the lid; this is how you will access the nest box in the winter to clean it out once a year, so attach two hinges at one side of the lid.

5 Fasten the hinges to the back of the box ensuring a snug fit. There—it really is that simple. Once you know what you are doing you could make several for around your backyard. They also make great gifts, and you can put surprises in them as well. For hanging details, see the following two pages.

Positioning your birdhouse

You have your birdhouse, now where do you nail it? Well it does depend a little on the species that you want to attract. But you have to get several factors right. Height is the first one, it needs to be high enough for the birds to feel secure—6 feet is a good height for most common garden birds. Shelter is also very important as no bird wants cold rain driving in their front door, so somewhere protected from the elements, the cold, wet, and sun is a good idea.

But on top of all this you have to balance the birds' requirements with "viewability," because it is always interesting to see the comings and goings of your residents. Experiment by putting up boxes in different locations and at different heights. Then be patient—some boxes do not seem suitable until they have weathered a season or two first. If you are still not having much luck, try another spot.

Positioning your nest is a compromise between the needs of the birds and the needs of the naturalist, who will want to keep an eye on things.

Take it further

* Now you have got the hang of making a bird box, you could try varying the size of the entrance holes to try to attract some different birds.
> 1¼ in: titmice/chickadees
> 1 in: Carolina wren
> 1½ in: bluebirds and tree swallows
> Cut the front in half: American robin, Eastern Phoebe.

* If you have a wooded and wild garden, you could try making owl or kestrel boxes, or even a special one for browncreepers; but this is getting a little specialized, so on page 70 there is more information.

Here is a classic wooden design of birdhouse, much tried and tested by birds and people, next to the latest thing in bird residencies: woodcrete. This strong mix of wood and concrete may be more expensive but it should last a lot longer than wood alone. Predators also find it hard to nibble and chisel through.

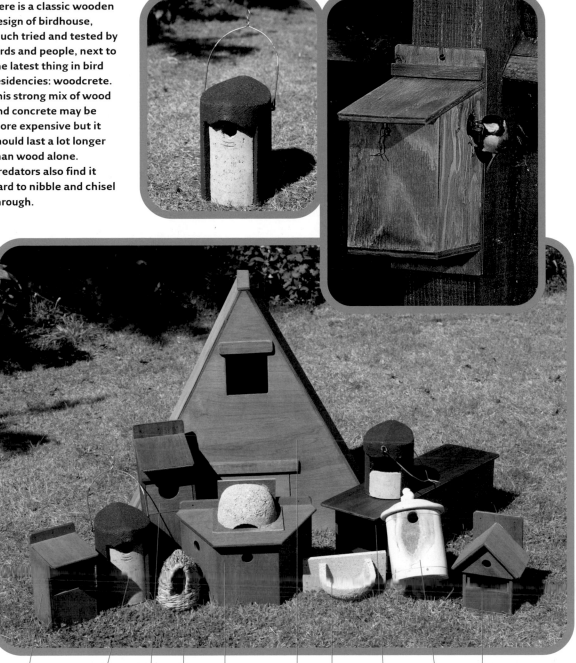

Phoebe/robin

Woodcrete chickadee box

Roosting pocket for wrens

Screech owl

House sparrow terrace

Barn owl

Barn swallow

American kestrel

House wren

Convertible box for open front and hole nester

Make a rain gauge

By catching and storing rainwater, you are helping to make the most of a valuable resource. You might want to put a water barrel in your garden so that you can store larger quantities. As much as 25,000 gallons of rain falls on the roof of your house each year, so if you connect it to the guttering from your roof, you will be able to collect a large amount.

Rainwater has far more nutrients and doesn't have the chemicals found in tap water, so it's better for a lot of creatures and plants. In fact, algae love rainwater so much that you will probably find your rainwater supply gets green and slimy pretty quickly.

To make the rain gauge opposite you will need to ask an adult to cut the bottom off an old plastic soda bottle and between you twist garden wire around it to make a support that can then be hung on a fence or other suitable place. Then follow the steps opposite for how to use your rain gauge.

Make sure there isn't anything sticking out over the top of the place you choose to hang your rain gauge. You must be able to catch the maximum amount of rain possible.

Fab fact

By the time your supply of rainwater is a few days old there will be hundreds of microscopic creatures living in it. In fact, the first microscope was invented in 1675 by a Dutch merchant called Anton van Leeuwenhoek, who discovered lots of living creatures in a pot of rainwater that had stood outside his house for a few days.

1   Tie a piece of string around the pillar or perhaps a tree trunk from which you will hang your gauge. If you are using a fence, bang in a nail. Tie a wire around the mouth of the plastic bottle.

2   Insert the metal loop at the top of the wire frame into the string support. Go away and wait for the rain to fall.

3   Either mark on the container the level of each day's rainfall—it might be easier to take the container out of the frame to do this— or ...

4   ... measure the amount of rainfall with a ruler and make a note of it—see also "Take it further" to the right.

Take it further

* Keep a log book of weekly or monthly rainfall.

* If you keep it going for a few years, you'll be able to see how the rainfall differs from year to year.

* You can also use a jar to see how much water is in snow. Put an inch of snow in a jar, then bring it inside and let it melt. Heavy wet snow will have a lot more water in it than dry fluffy snow.

Fluff and stuff for nest building

Even before the spring gets going properly, garden birds are already starting to rummage around securing nest sites and preparing for the approaching nesting season. It is at this time of the year that birds have special needs. They have to make nests to insulate their brood and stop their eggs from rolling around, and for that they need building materials.

You can turn your backyard into a nest maker's store and at the same time have a little fun, not only by watching the birds trying to transport the stuff to the nest, but also by watching which species use what materials. The rules are similar to feeding the birds, try offering a variety of materials in different ways. To make a nest bag, see the steps opposite.

YOU WILL NEED

> **old sock or stocking**
> **mixture of nesting materials (see Step 1)**
> **string**
> **scissors**

1 This is a great way of using mom's old tights or even that odd sock that seems to have lost its partner in the wash. Collect a variety of materials, such as dried grass, straw, hay, feathers, and wool. Add some animal hair and wool collected from barbed wire fences or from your dog or cat's grooming brush, and even from your hair brush! All these things make excellent materials for different birds to weave into nests.

2 Spread out your collection on some plates so you can take your pick of which items you will stuff into the sock or tights. Look at an old nest in the winter and you will see some are lined with mud and moss and finished with a warm, fluffy layer of fine grass, wool, hair, and feathers designed to keep the eggs and the chicks cozy.

3 Start stuffing your stocking or sock, making sure you get a good mixture of the materials, pushing them right down to the foot.

4 Separate the different materials by either twisting and knotting the stocking or tying off portions of the sock with string.

5 Cut little holes in the sock and pull some of the stuffing through to allow the birds to see what's on offer. Go and hang the sock somewhere where you can see it and watch and wait.

Take it further

* Because most nests are built of different kinds of material and many birds have their own favorites, you may need to provide other stuff, too. As well as using the sock method, you can put on a nest builder's buffet.

* Collect a selection of shallow bowls and trays and in each put a different building material, try a big tray of wet mud and you might get swallows coming down to collect it. Robins, phoebes, and even potter wasps may also visit the buffet table.

* Moss is also used by many species and coarser straw, and fine sticks and twigs may be taken away by everything from mourning doves to bluejays.

Homes and holes

This chapter is all about providing a comfortable home for your wildlife and the great thing is that it doesn't matter if you have a window box or a postage stamp for a backyard, you can still create a habitat or two, even if it is just a small one. Little habitats are homes to little things and lots of little habitats make up one bigger one!

Providing food is a way of attracting wildlife to your backyard and once you have achieved that, the challenge is to get your visitors to stay. There is a huge range of products out there on the market—homes and houses for everything from ladybirds and toads to bees and bats—and even though there are plenty of addresses on pages 70-1 for various supply companies, many of the basics can be made at home very inexpensively. Sometimes it doesn't even require much creativity. A weed patch or an area of long grass, for example, may look untidy to you, but it will provide more homes and hideouts for wildlife than you might at first imagine.

The lawn can look like a great big green desert spread out in front of your house. No good but to play baseball on, right? Well, we humans have a habit of raking and tidying up this carpet of grass, but it can provide a home for that king of wigglers, the intestines of the soil—the worms. They are not only good for the garden soil—turning it, aerating it, and fertilizing it—they will also provide indirectly much food for many mammals and birds. In turn, this provides entertainment for us naturalists.

The other backyard desert, concrete, is also hard to imagine as being much of a habitat, but inevitably it cracks and in these yawning canyons a colony of ants can fit. The concrete works as a giant storage heater, giving protection from the elements and providing the ideal base for these gardeners' friends to base their exploits.

Wild grass attracts insects and small mammals.

Worm heaven.

Small holes will attract many an insect such as wasps and beetles.

Between each paving stone lurk hundreds of ants.

A bat box is a larger home that you can make yourself.

Make a bumblebee box

Bumblebees are round and furry. They pollinate our flowers and fruit trees and, they remind us of happy times, because they are among the first of the insects in the spring to brave the cold weather. They are able to do this because they have a special way of dislocating their wings and revving their big flight muscles to generate body heat (a bit like our shivering).

You can make your garden a haven for these little fluffballs by creating some nest sites for them. In the wild, they usually use the old burrows of mice or similar dark, dry crevices. This is what the queens are doing when they first emerge in the spring and you can watch them searching any dark hole. This is the time of year you need to get your bumblebee box out if you are to stand any chance of a queen moving in.

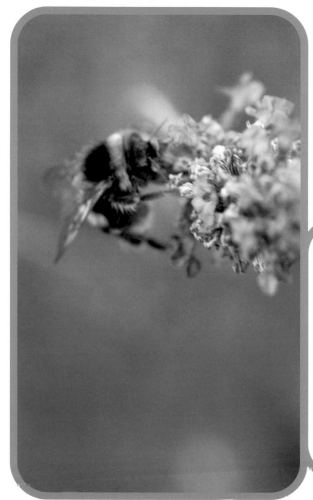

If you are providing nest boxes for bees, why not provide them with food too—in the form of nectar-rich flowers.

Take my advice

* Bees can be fickle and fussy so to increase your chances, make a few nests and try them in different positions.

* Keep an eye on your nests for coming and going bee action. This will tell you that you have a colony starting up.

* Make your garden super bee friendly by planting a variety of nectar-rich flowers

YOU WILL NEED

> 6-8 inch wide plastic flower pot with one hole in the center (although see Step 5 if yours has more)
> trowel
> 12 x 12 inch piece of wire mesh
> nesting material such as moss, hay, coarse straw
> 8 inch standard hosepipe

1 There is not much making required here; all you need to do is choose a sunny location—south facing is ideal—and dig a hole deep enough and the right shape to fit your chosen pot upside down. This doesn't have to be on level ground, it could be in a bank.

2 Take the wire mesh and put a big fist full of nesting material in the center of it.

3 Scrunch up the wire mesh—be very careful of any sharp pieces that might be sticking out the side—so that the bedding material is safely enclosed. Push the bundle into the flower pot.

4 Turn the flower pot upside down and put into your freshly dug hole. Push the hose into the central drainage hole in the bottom—now the top!—of the flower pot. This will become the entrance for the bees.

5 Cover any extra holes with stones and return the soil around and over the pot. Surround the entrance with stones or logs to give the bees some privacy and wait for a questing queen to stick her head in. Always observe your potential colony from a safe distance.

The "embryo" nest

Just the sight of a wasp's yellow-and-black striped uniform sends many of us into an arm-flapping panic. Social wasps—such as hornets or yellow jackets—are much feared, mainly because they have the ability to get our attention by using their sharp and venom-loaded sting. But get past this and you will be surprised by what you will find.

They are actually one of my favorite creatures; colorful, interesting, great pollinators of flowers and fruit trees and, of course, something that gets overlooked. They are, in fact, brilliant and efficient predators of many garden pests such as caterpillars, bugs, and spiders. It's a shame that the sting gets in the way.

If you want to witness the beauty of a wasps' nest without the threatening presence of thousands of workers, look around in the winter. Good places to search are in loft spaces, garden sheds, and in woods once the leaves have fallen. However, always be very careful indeed when inspecting nests—wasps can be very aggressive and sting when disturbed.

The remarkable thing about a wasps' nest is that as the colony swells, the "skin" can be recycled, rewetted, and remolded into new shapes.

Fab fact

When freezing temperatures set in—usually in the late fall or early winter—the wasps' nest falls to pieces and all the workers die. The new queens who would have now mated need to find a place to hibernate. It is their task to carry on through this hard time of the year, so they can start again from scratch when it grows warmer again in the spring. Look for these new queens under bark or in any cool dry place. You can tell if your wasp is hibernating because it will be very still, hanging on with its jaws, and its wings will be folded down. Don't worry, she will be very sleepy, so just watch from a safe distance and then leave her be.

Remember that there are different types of social wasps. The common paper wasp is less harmful than the yellow jacket and hornet and is easily observed, as it is widespread across the United States. In early spring you may stumble across the early stages of a queen's labors. You are looking for a very fragile, golf ball-shaped thing, usually creamy white to gray in color, suspended from the ceiling. This is the beginnings of a nest that could get to be a foot or more across in size by the end of the year!

When a nest is at this stage, it is usually only tended by the queen. As her first batch of daughters have not yet grown up, she starts off doing everything herself, building the first cluster of brood cells and wrapping the entire thing in a fragile envelope of "paper" made from chewed wood. She also feeds the grubs, and incubates them once they have hatched by curling her body around the base of the cells.

If you find one of these strange fruits, the first thing to do is to find out whether or not the insect is in it. Many nests get abandoned at this stage because either the queen wasp decides she's made a bad decision in her nest location, or she dies or is killed. Because she has a lot on her plate, she may well be out foraging during the day. At night, however, she will return to her home, so it is at this time that you should gently approach the nest with a flashlight and try looking up into the nest through the entrance hole to see if she is in.

Keep an eye out and an ear open for wasps rasping away at fence posts, sheds, gates, and benches. They are getting a good mandible full of wood fiber, which they combine with their saliva to make a pulp. This is then used to build their nests.

Take it further

* If the queen has abandoned her nest and you are sure she has not returned, you can collect the nest and look at it close up.

* Look for the different-colored bands of "paper" on the outside, each representing a different source of wood fiber.

* Try cutting the envelope in half with scissors to show the structure inside.

Nice pile for the wildlife

One of the easiest ways to provide accommodation for wildlife is to make a log pile. There's not much making involved, I know, as logs have been designed so that you just have to pile them up! Choose a good mixture of wood types and stack them, if possible, in a warm, sunny, south-facing spot.

Why does this attract wildlife? Well, dead wood is nearly always cleared up or burnt in our very tidy and organized world, especially in the yard, but in the wild this is a very popular habitat. Not only do some creatures eat it, but it provides many damp hiding holes, also, and your log pile will do all these things and more.

You can further improve your log pile by doing some basic woodwork and using a drill to put holes of various sizes in the logs. These will provide shelters for small insects. You can also try making simple small boxes, like birdhouses but even smaller. Put a small round hole in one side and you will be providing a snug hide-out for anything from a homeless small mammal to a frog or toad. The bigger the pile and the more artificial burrows, the better.

Even the tiniest of disturbances by the feet and tails of the smallest of rodents and even invertebrates, such as beetles and millipedes, can be recorded in detail by using smoked glass or china. Provided you can protect the surface from rain and debris, this is a great way of finding out exactly what is living in your log pile (see opposite).

3 You will quickly get interesting tracks where animals scuff and scrape off the thin layer of carbon with their activities. It may take some imagination and interpretation to guess what creatures have made which tracks. You may also get so much activity that all you see is a jumble of traces that make no sense. Play, experiment, and adapt and, with luck, you will get some very beautiful works of art.

2 Place the plate in a sheltered place with the carbon side facing upward. If you wish it to be used by small mammals, you can try baiting it and covering it with a makeshift shelter, such as an old roof slate balanced on stones.

1 Take an old plate and hold it over the flame of a candle, taking great care not to get your hands too near the flame. Keep moving the plate and don't hold it too close to the flame, as china has a tendency to crack if it gets too hot. What you want is for an even layer of black carbon to be deposited on the surface.

Take it further

If you get something you want to keep, spray with hair spray or fixative and peel off the plate. Then display it with a back light, such as in a window.

Homes for the hairy

Bats live a secret life more hidden away than most other wild mammals. Because of this, most of us will have almost no idea about what bats live in in our area or even what they look like up close. OK, so they don't make it easy for themselves, being small, active after dark and fast flying. As a result, few of us get a chance to experience the battiness of bats.

But if things continue the way they are, there will not be any bats left. They would have quietly squeaked their last high-frequency squeak with nobody listening or even noticing. One of the big problems they face is a lack of habitat. Bats traditionally roost in old trees, root holes, cavities, and caves. They will also use railway tunnels and roof spaces, but sadly these are increasingly disappearing.

Old trees and dead wood are less tolerated and fall down; we spray our building timbers with toxic chemicals to stop them rotting (great for lengthening the life of a house but lethal to bats); and we either block up or go exploring in caves and so disturb other roost sites. As a result, bat accommodation is scarce and one of the best ways to help out your local ones is to make your own roost sites— otherwise known as bat boxes (see opposite).

Once finished, site your box as high as you can. Asking a grown-up to go up a ladder is good, so that the box will be well out of the way of cats and other predators. A tree is best but you can put it on a building as well. If on a tree, it is a good idea to put up three of them, facing north, southeast, and southwest. This gives the bats choice in different weather conditions. They also like a clear flight path, so choose a tree without too many branches obstructing the box.

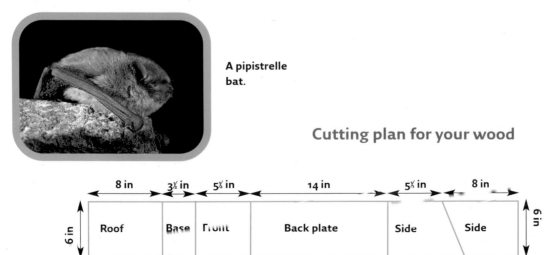

A pipistrelle bat.

Cutting plan for your wood

8 in	3⅛ in	5⅛ in	14 in	5⅛ in	8 in
Roof	Base	Front	Back plate	Side	Side

6 in

1

Cut up your plank according to the dimensions on the diagram. On the back plate, use the chisel to cut a groove that is ⅛ in deep, 1 in wide and 2 in from the top. Then start piecing the box together. Nail the front to the base. Then nail the sides first to the front piece ...

2

... and then to the back. You should have a gap of ¼–1 in at the bottom between the base and back, which is how the bats get in and out of their box.

3

If your wood is not rough sawn, then rough it up. Scratch the surface with a nail, especially on the inside. Think about how bats move around. They like to hang on and clamber about with their tiny clawed feet and fingers, so they need a good grippy surface if they are to move around inside your box.

4

Screw down the lid so that nothing will disturb your bats. But if you ever need to clean out the box, you can remove the screws. It is against the law to disturb your bats, even if you have given them somewhere to live.

5

It isn't easy to know for sure if you have bats. Keep an eye at a distance and you may start noticing a stain by the entrance. Of course, if you watch carefully on a summer evening, you may see your bats flitting around. Whatever you do, resist the temptation to take a peek.

Seeking secretive backyard critters

Your backyard may be home to a surprising variety of wildlife, even if you live in a big city. Species such as raccoons, opossums, and skunks are often more common in cities and suburbs than they are in the countryside, where we tend to think wild animals "belong." Even larger predators like foxes and coyotes can make a good living in our yards and gardens. Can you figure out why this might be? Be careful never to trap any wild animals, and always keep a safe distance when observing them.

Wild animals don't see the difference between "wild" and "civilized" the way we tend to. They just focus on the things that are important to them, mainly a reliable food supply and good places to make their dens. Now think about a woodland that you are familiar with and compare it to your neighborhood. Which do you think has more food of various kinds available and more places that make good dens?

Seeing backyard wildlife—except for birds—can be quite hard, despite the fact that it is common. One reason is that many animals are active only at night.

So how can you see this stuff? The simplest "trick" is simply to look in the right place at the right time. Lots of animals start to forage just as it's beginning to get dark, so this is a good time to explore. Use caution when viewing animals. Don't lift up rocks or fallen tree limbs with your hands but use a stick since potentially dangerous animals can live under these things.

Making your yard more "wildlife friendly" will help a lot. Persuade your parents to let part of your yard get a little wilder than the rest—let some grass and weeds grow up and add a few rocks and a log.

A small mammal such as an opossum, gopher, shrew or rabbit might be attracted to your backyard.

2 Try to pick different "micro-habitats," or create some habitat by collecting some dead leaves and putting them under one of the boards.

3 Leave it alone for a week or so and then check underneath to see what has come along—maybe sowbugs, a salamander, or even a snake.

1 A super-simple way to attract some interesting animals to your yard is to put a few sheets of plywood—2 feet by 3 feet is a good size—in different parts of your yard.

See if you can spot a chipmunk like this one in your yard. They search for nuts, berries, and seeds, and although they live in burrows, they also climb up trees.

Small mammal observation box

If you live somewhere where there do not appear to be any larger mammals, then what about these small ones? And before you get all squeamish about rats and mice and all the annoying things they are supposed to do, just remember that they have managed to survive alongside us and exploit our own untidy habits. So they deserve a little bit more thought than most people would tend to give them.

But in addition to species that your local exterminator will try to convince you are vermin, you can also attract many other "nice" and truly wild and native species of small mammals such as voles, squirrels, and chipmunks. All you need to do is adapt the principle of a bird table—I call it a mammal box—and here is how to make one. This works best if you have French-style or patio doors. Use caution when viewing the animals. Always keep a safe distance.

Voles are one of several common species of small mammal that can be attracted to your observation box.

Cutting plan for your wood

3 Take the plastic pipes and scratch the insides with an old nail or, if you can't do this, run a piece of rope or string on the inside. Both of these ideas will encourage the mammals to climb up the pipes. Push the plastic pipes into the holes on the sides. Make sure the animals don't get trapped.

2 Screw together the pieces in the following order:
* Screw sides to base with holes toward the bottom.
* Screw back to base and sides.
* Screw top to base and sides (as photographed).
You then have a box with a top, bottom, two sides, and a back, but no front.

1 Ask an adult to help you cut out the pieces of wood, following the diagram opposite. Drill some drainage holes on the bottom. Also cut holes for where you want your plastic pipes to enter the box.

4 Then all you need do is position your mammal observation box up against a window, bait and wait. Once a mammal appears, try looking at it with a desk lamp containing a red light bulb. The bulb shouldn't startle your visitor and slowly you can bring it closer to the box and enjoy what you see.

Tracking wildlife in your backyard

Once you are settled down in front of the TV in the evening, watching your favorite show, you would be surprised at what creatures come out of hiding within your neighborhood. Even deep in the city, eyes are opening and whiskers are twitching as the night shift wakes up and goes about its business. But without staying up and mounting an all-night vigil, how do you get to know what's been going on? Well, here are a few tricks and techniques to help you piece together the secret activities of your surprising neighbors.

You may find the odd dropping on your lawn or at the edge of your garden shrubbery, but if you simply wrinkle your nose and ignore it, you will be passing up a real treasure trove of information. Now, you may not get that excited by the prospect of dung, but for many mammals this is often the closest you can get. Without going into identification of droppings in great detail (this is a job for another book), you can tell an awful lot if you look at them through the right eyes. Ask yourselves the following questions: How big is it? What's it made of? What is its shape and where is it?

When looking at the size, its width will immediately give you a clue to the size of the animal's bottom, which, odd though this may seem, in most cases is related to the overall size of the animal!

Then have a close look to see what it's made of, but be careful not to get your face too close. Use a stick or something to break the dropping apart and you may get a clue as to what the animal has been eating. Look out for traces of bone, fur, plant seeds, and fibers and the hard bits of insects, as these obviously tell you what was for dinner but also who was doing the eating. For example, a twisted dropping with fur and bones was made by a wild carnivore while a fibrous pellet was produced by a herbivorous mammal.

The tubular, twisted shape of this dropping, as well as evidence of fur and bone in the dropping, say that a fox has passed through the backyard.

Some droppings are very distinctive in their form. Rabbits and deer produce pellets that are dropped randomly, while badgers in Europe leave their droppings in little pits. Foxes like placing theirs in high-up and obvious places, like on top of stones or at the edges of paths.

If you have a suspicious hole in a hedge, or an obvious "run" (which looks like a path through long grass) that crosses your garden, there are a few ways you can work out who uses them.

Prints of some common garden visitors: fox and dog can be hard to tell apart.

Take it further

* We all know that soft ground like sand or mud is best for preserving footprints, so even if your garden is a little short of damp areas, you can create your own by making a "tracking bed." You need a tray and fine damp sand or mud (mixed up from soil and water; clay is even better).

* Simply put your soft stuff in the tray and put this on or along the animal's "run." The best position is somewhere where the animal cannot bypass the tracking bed and walk around it. So right next to the hole in the hedge is ideal.

* Use your imagination in any way you can to try to get the mysterious creature to put its foot in it!

Unless you are really lucky, the only cat print you are likely to find is of the domesticated variety. But it's worth noting so you can tell others apart.

This delicate hand is the distinctive front foot print of a raccoon.

Creepy crawlies

Those small creatures that the rest of the world likes to refer to as creepy crawlies are almost universally unloved at worst, or at best simply ignored. As humans we see the whole world from around the same height as our head! So things we look up to impress us, and little things we look down at tend not to. The creepy crawlies suffer twice because on top of their small size many are often totally misunderstood. This is partly due to the fact that we don't know what they actually are and also because some of them make us feel afraid, even if they are totally harmless.

 Dare yourself to look at a spider or an ant through a magnifying glass and you will be surprised at what you see. Even if it doesn't change how you feel about these animals and they still send you running off screaming, at least you will be more aware of what makes them what they are. You will at least be aware that they are more than just a dot with legs!

The other thing I like about insects and other invertebrates is that they are small; I know I may be stating the obvious here, but when you are small you do not need a lot of space. Nor do you need a lot of food. So it doesn't matter how small or desolate your space is, you will always find insect life. This is one of the reasons they are some of the most successful creatures on Earth.

They are also cheap to attract and study. Simply by leaving out a bit of old carpet, a small tub of water, or planting a nectar-producing flowering plant in a corner, you will be creating a home for something or other!

The big, fat female orb-weaving spider is a common sight in the summer, sitting plumb in the middle of a classic spider's web.

Every home—even those at the top of high rises—will have ants patrolling the walls or pavements.

These popular beetles may add a splash of color to the garden, but the reds and oranges are more than just pretty colors. They tell of poisons and toxins, which make ladybirds inedible to many birds and other creatures.

They might be much feared beasts, but earwigs cannot hurt you. They may nibble your mom's chrysanthemums, but the pincers that make them easily recognizable are used only for fighting and folding up their wings.

Butterfly baiting

I guess it's similar to feeding the birds, but providing a menu for any wildlife is one of the first steps to attracting them, and feeding butterflies and other insects is no exception. The way to a butterfly's loyalty is via its proboscis, and by this I mean you have to give them nectar-rich flowers for the adults to feed on. Alternatively, you can put out sweet food for them to feast on (see pages 48-9).

Get out into the surrounding wild spaces and look at what butterflies and other insects are attracted to and what species of flowers thrive in the soil around your area. Usually there are favorites that produce copious quantities of the sweet stuff—such as milkweeds, mints, and other herbs—and these always seem to have a host of winged things buzzing around them.

Different kinds of butterflies fly at different times of year. If you have something in bloom from early spring through fall, you can attract a maximum variety of species to your backyard.

The buddleia or butterfly bush is a magnet for many species. Just plant your bush, wait for it to flower and watch the insects come flocking in. By putting your bush in a sunny spot, you make it even more irresistible to the butterflies and bees.

> **buddleia plant**
> **glass**
> **sun**

2 Place the shoot in water on a window sill or just stick it straight in the ground.

3 Very quickly it will grow roots and start sprouting.

1 If buying a buddleia is more than your budget can handle, take cuttings. Be sure to ask for permission if the plant is in someone's backyard. This is a quick and simple way to grow plants without having to sow seeds, and buddleia is easier than most other plants. Peel away a shoot from the main plant close to where it is attached. It should come away with a "foot" on it. Remove any leaves that are near it.

Take it further

* The adult stage is only a quarter of a butterfly's life cycle, so once you have lured the adults and they are happily flitting about in your bushes and borders, the next step is to make them stay. To do this you need to provide food and conditions that the often fussier egg, caterpillar, and chrysalis stage require.

* For the more common species, this can be as simple as providing a wild area of long grass. A patch of milkweed in a sunny place will attract many species and monarchs may lay their eggs on the leaves. Black swallowtails lay eggs on members of the carrot family and many skippers feed on grasses.

* Do your research, make your observations and plant accordingly. You will make a lot of caterpillars and other insects very happy. Once you have happy insects, you will have the beginnings of a happy habitat for all manner of other species.

Butterfly bar

Not all butterflies prefer to feed at flowers. Mourning cloaks, commas and tortoiseshells would rather drink sap or the juices of rotting fruit; these butterflies spend the winter in the adult stage.

In the garden, these butterflies are often attracted to rotten fruit. I have a plum tree near me which is in a sunny hot spot. The fruit ferments on the branches and the local comma butterflies can be found feeding here almost until the first frosts of winter. Other favorite feeding places are on windfall apples and pears. But if you don't have any of these natural sources of fruit, you can attract the insects with your own "butterfly bar."

Once your have your bar up and running, sit and watch to see who comes to visit. In addition to the butterflies, you may also get wasps and yellow jackets, so it is probably best to put your bar as far away from other people and houses as possible. But at the same time, do not turn down the opportunity to see these, some of my favorite and least understood insects, up close (see also pages 32–3).

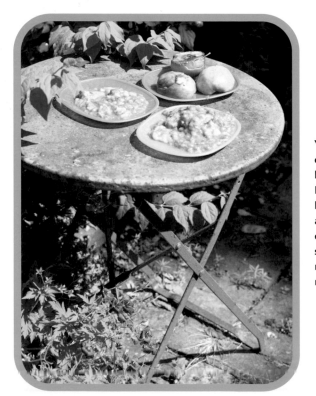

You have created a butterfly bar. It's rather like a large version of a flower—lots of color and a sweet, sugary reward in the middle!

2
Mash up the fruit in a bowl and, if necessary, add a little water to make it good and runny. Then add some brown sugar.

3
Dish up your fine mixture on a plate or two and leave out in the garden to attract all those hungry butterflies.

1
Just collect some old soft fruit—maybe your local farm stand has some spoilt stock that you can have. Bananas, apples, grapes, peaches, plums, and pears are all good.

The comma and mourning cloak butterflies are two species that are on the wing from early spring to late fall and will then hibernate as adult butterflies. Because of this, they need sugar to build up their body fat reserves to see them through the cold months.

The shape shifters

We tend to take the life cycles of some of our garden insects a little bit for granted. That of the butterflies and moths is no exception; just think about it for a moment and look at the sequence of pictures opposite.

But this miracle is by no means exclusive and can be readily seen within the confines of a slightly modified box, bottle, or empty fish tank. You can even buy a butterfly or moth kit by mail order and see for yourself a caterpillar changing to a chrysalis and then to a butterfly.

You can rear many different species of caterpillar (see opposite) as long as you either see for yourself what food plant they are eating or are able to identify the type of caterpillar. Keep a record of the caterpillars and the adult moth or butterfly. A digital camera makes this very easy.

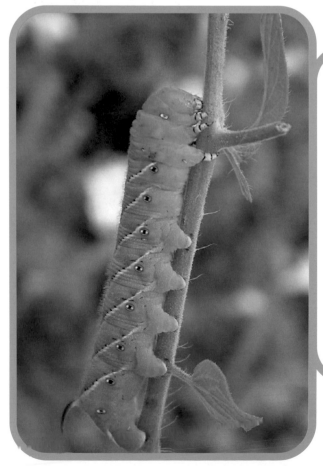

Fab facts

* If you are really lucky, you will be able to catch the emergence of a butterfly or moth from its chrysalis. This often happens in the dark, early in the morning, as in the wild they would be very vulnerable at this time and in this way they can avoid any predators.

* Some of the big hawk moths and silk moths put on around 27,000 times their original hatching weight!

* Caterpillars shed their skins up to nine times in their short lives.

YOU WILL NEED

> caterpillars
> cardboard box, sweet jar, old plastic soda bottle, or jam jar with a lid
> kitchen paper
> fresh food from the garden
> twigs

1 The butterfly's cycle begins as an egg, a speck of life out of which hatches a little soft, squishy, worm-like creature. This is a caterpillar and it's born with an enormous appetite. Collect your own from among chomped leaves in the backyard. If you look carefully, caterpillars can be found almost anywhere.

2 Put your caterpillars in your chosen container lined with a piece of kitchen paper—and always add a lid with air holes pierced in it. Feed them plenty of fresh food. This should be the same plant type as you found them on, as many caterpillars are fussy eaters and will starve to death rather than eat the wrong food. Thoroughly clean the container every few days.

3 Supply them with branched twigs for the day they settle down to change. When they reach a certain size, caterpillars molt and underneath is no caterpillar but an odd-shaped case, called a pupa or chrysalis. Do not disturb the chrysalides.

4 After about ten days the pupa start to change color, which means it is about to split and reveal a magnificent and beautifully colored butterfly or moth.

Little leaf lovers

In summer you may notice that some of the leaves on the trees and bushes in your park or garden have developed a strange wiggly pattern on them. Well, look closely and you will see that this pattern is not actually on the leaves but inside them.

These feats of micro-engineering are the tunnels of leaf miners, tiny micro moths, the adults of which are probably among the least noticeable and unassuming creatures in your garden. It makes sense, if you are small enough to fit between the two surfaces of a leaf, that this would be a fairly safe haven from most predators.

Backlight the tunnels of a leaf miner with a bright flashlight and you can see their work and sometimes even the insect inside.

The same principle works if you tape the leaf to a window. Look at how the tunnel starts off narrow and, as the caterpillar gets bigger and fatter, so does its tunnel.

2 Another way to clearly see the miner at work is to tape the leaf to a window. You should be able to see the activities of your miners from indoors.

3 Look through the magnifying glass from your handy stuff (see pages 6-7) and you will see all sorts of details not noticed by the naked eye.

1 Place a small flashlight behind your leaf and search the tunnels for the miner itself. You will probably see lots of droppings, but follow the tunnel to its end and here you will be able to see the silhouette of a small caterpillar. If it isn't moving, the chances are it has turned into a pupa and is waiting to hatch. If this is the case, collect the leaf and keep it in a small airtight plastic box and watch and wait to see what comes out.

Take it further

* Place a branch of leaves containing miners in a jug of water on your window sill and keep a record of their progress— but first promise your parents that you will clean the windows once your experiment is over! Using a marker, mark and plot each day's activity. Notice how the tunnel gets wider as the caterpillar inside grows fatter.

* When your miner has left the leaf, keep your mine by pressing the leaf on kitchen paper within the pages of a big book.

* There are many kinds of leaf miner. See how many you can find. Are they loyal to certain species of tree? Do different species make different-shaped mines?

Suckers for the sweet stuff

Now, if you think butterflies have a secret life then you will find their nocturnal cousins, the moths, positively mysterious. During the daylight hours, they tend not to draw attention to themselves by keeping a very low profile. This is further helped by the fact that they are very well camouflaged. But when we are at our least active, they are at their most active.

If you want to learn about the moths you have living around you, there is a rather fun and sticky way to get to know some of them. It relies on the fact that many moths fuel their activities in the same way as butterflies by feeding on sweet, sugary liquid. This can be nectar from flowers, but just as easily it can be sap oozing from wounded plant stems, or even rotten and fermenting fruit. It seems the sweeter it is, the more they love it.

You can take advantage of this behavior by serving up your own sweet and sticky meal that is all dessert and no first course. It is a technique that lepidopterists (that's the name for someone who studies butterflies and moths) have been using for hundreds of years and is called "sugaring."

Underwing moths, named for their bristly colored hind wings, are among the many striking species attracted by sugaring.

Fab fact

When you do see your moths, spend a little time watching how they are feeding. See how their eyes glow in an eerie way as they reflect your flashlight back at you.

> sweet food, e.g. syrup, honey, sugar, fruit juice
> small amount of Coca Cola
> saucepan
> wooden spoon
> old sock or piece of rope
> string
> flashlight

3 At dusk, hang your sock in a tree, from the washing line, over the backyard fence— or anywhere else you choose. Then leave for a few hours and return after dark with a flashlight to see who has turned up.

2 When you are happy with your culinary creation, you now need to start thinking about how to serve it up. You can make "moth socks" or you can use rope. If you are using a sock, tie a piece of string around the top and then put the sock (or rope, if using) into the mixture before it cools down. Stir it around.

1 Put all the sweet ingredients in the saucepan and slowly heat until everything has dissolved. Add a little of the Coca Cola. This helps give your mixture a great fermenting smell that will waft far and wide and tantalize the antennae of moths for miles around!

4 Alternatively, make your mixture a little stickier by adding more sugar at the mixing stage. Paint it onto trees and fence posts in and around the garden and then, as for Step 3, come back when it's dark with your flashlight to see what visitors you have encouraged.

Beguiled by bulbs

Moths are famous for being attracted to bright lights. The old saying, "Like moths to a flame" not only applies to candles and fire; moths also find the modern equivalent just as mesmerizing.

When I was a budding young naturalist I had very little pocket money to play with—even my paper round if I did it for a year wouldn't cover the cost of a good professional moth trap. So I came up with my own solution—changing my bedroom into a giant moth trap.

Stay up after dark and turn on all the lights in your bedroom and keep the curtains or blinds open. After an hour or two you will start to see various moths turning up on your window and even the occasional large beetle will come whirring by, bouncing noisily off the panes of glass.

Some of the moths will settle and stay still, which will allow you to see them up close and inspect them through the window with a magnifying glass. The only problem is that seeing their top side is the best way of actually identifying them and to do this you have to open the window and let them in. But do this and you will run the risk of making yourself very unpopular with your family—especially when you let in all the neighborhood mosquitoes and midges as well.

Fab fact

Why do so many nocturnal insects get drawn to light? Well there has to be a reason, but why this common behavior occurs is one of those real mysteries of nature. One of the best theories is that moths use natural light such as the moon and the stars to navigate in a straight line. Because these lights are far away, this works, but when the lights are closer to them—our artificial electric moons and stars—these become a bit of a distraction and cause them to fly in ever decreasing circles until they are head butting the bulb!

The luna moth is one of the most spectacular moths you are likely to see.

The Virgo Tiger moth is one of our prettiest species.

Take it further

* If you find that you start getting seriously into moths, there are a few cheaper types of proper moth traps available and this would make a pretty fantastic birthday or holiday gift.

* The trap featured here is a basic, affordable and portable trap. It is perfect for beginners and the way it works is very straightforward.

The tube light attracts the moth, which then falls down into the collection box full of egg cartons.

* If you get really serious, you may decide it is time to spend much more money on a very high quality one.

Plant bugs

What is an aphid? Well, these tiny little sap-sucking insects may be well known to gardeners who continually wage war against them as they mount their annual attack on rose bushes and other plants every summer. But to the rest of us?

That sticky stuff that covers your car windshield if you park under the wrong species of tree in the summer is honey dew. This is a pleasant phrase for the excrement that is produced by aphids. To find out a bit more about what honey dew is, how it is used and produced, there is a little demonstration you can do (see opposite).

Once caught, look through a magnifying glass at the head end of the aphid and you will notice the straw-like mouth parts that it stabs into plant stems and uses to tap the neverending flow of sap. As the liquid passes through its body, the aphid takes what it needs and the rest drops onto the leaf and creates a habitat for molds. Ants may feed on it, too, and sometimes it is so plentiful that it drops out of the tree and gets stuck on the windscreen of any car parked beneath.

Fab fact

In two months, a single aphid can, in theory, give rise to six million new aphids! With figures like this if they were all to survive, there would be no point gardening. But fortunately many creatures rely on them as food, including wasps, ladybirds, lacewings, and many bird populations.

1

Either find a sacrificial pot plant that already has a population of greenfly or black fly (other names for aphids), or forage around in the garden for an unfortunate plant that is being sucked dry. Cut yourself a branch or stem and put this in water.

2

To stop infecting every other plant in the house—something that plant-loving moms and dads would not be too happy about—remove all the insects with wings with a pair of tweezers or a toothpick stick into a bowl and take outside. Now you are ready to observe the secrets of your herds in the herbaceous border.

3

Scrutinize the colony through a magnifying glass and you will notice insects of varying sizes. The biggest ones will be the adult females. These reproduce at an incredible rate as they do not need a male to mate with. They are simply baby factories and they produce clones of themselves, churning out up to ten a day. Inside these babies there will already be more babies developing!

Take it further

* Although these bugs look completely defenceless, they do have a number of escape tactics. The first can be seen if you tickle a colony with a paintbrush. A lot of them simply let go of the twig or bud on which they are feeding.

* Some will also present their rear end to an attacker and ooze a waxy substance out of the two tubes on either side of their abdomen. Called siphunculi (or honey dew), this is sticky and unpleasant, especially as it solidifies on the mouth parts or the eyes of a ladybird. If you watch a ladybird going about its business, it often has to stop to clean itself of this gunk.

The "wig" trap

Many insects are thigmatropic, which means they "love to squeeze their bodies into impossibly tight spaces." They do this as a safety measure because tight spaces are hard to access for most predators. Also, if you are a small invertebrate, the chances are the shelter provided helps prevent the loss of moisture through exposure.

Among their number are creatures such as the instantly recognizable earwig. If you look at one from the side, you will see it looks rather flattened, which means it can jam itself into small gaps. Other creatures that have similar habits are cockroaches and woodlice. The enterprising naturalist can make the most of this behavior by making an earwig trap.

There are several good designs, but one of the best is that used by some growers of prize show flowers, who are not too keen on earwigs, because of their habit of sitting in chrysanthemum flowers and having a nibble. The steps opposite show you how to make one in the same way.

Tell Mr and Mrs Wig apart: this one is a male as he has a much larger set of pincers on the end of his abdomen.

YOU WILL NEED

> **old flower pot**
> **stick**
> **straw or grass**
> **runny honey**
> **spoon**

2
Dribble lots of honey onto the straw and then, very carefully, so that you don't spill the honey onto your clothes ...

3
... turn the earwig trap upside down and push the stick into the ground at your chosen spot. A good place is somewhere that is lightly shaded.

1
Take the flower pot and stand your stick up in the center. Then stuff the straw or grass around the stick.

4
The next day, come back with a plastic container and investigate the contents of your trap to see what you've caught.

Take it further

* Variations on this earwig trap are made by using old rags or bits of carpet screwed up and draped over branches.

* Or make up rolls of corrugated cardboard and leave in similar dark places.

Rulers of the patio

The patio is where it all started for me. Getting down on my hands and knees and watching the frantic wars and struggles of the ants, their efficient foraging and fascinating dramas all acted out at a tiny scale right in front of my nose, was quite amazing. The little insights I gained from this Lilliputian world made me look at nature through completely different eyes. Follow the experiments below and opposite and you, too, will soon learn a lot about ants.

Nick's trick

Try to persuade an ant returning to the nest to walk over a sheet of glass or Plexiglas. As soon as it has obliged, sprinkle some talcum powder on the glass and blow off the excess. What you will just be able to see is a faint line of talc where it has stuck to the liquid the ant has oozed out of its bottom. This is a neat trick, but it doesn't work well with all species and some ants will leave better and juicier trails. Try it.

Fab fact

An ant has two tiny stomachs. The contents of the second one is shared with the rest of the colony—a kind of community stomach!

YOU WILL NEED

> black plastic garbage bag
> duct tape
> scissors
> honey or jam
> teaspoon

2 What you can't see is that the ant is dragging its bottom, leaving a trail of perfume. This is produced by a special organ known as the dufours gland. When an ant returns to the nest it shares samples of its find with its nest mates, who then set off back along the scent trail to the bait.

3 Soon you will notice the numbers start to increase around the food. Each ant returning to the nest does the same thing, and the numbers being recruited to the bait just keep swelling. In this way, the tiny ants can use the strength of their numbers to exploit any food they find. As the food runs out, the ants will return to the nest without food and the excitement starts to wane. The scent trail is not reinforced and it eventually dries up and evaporates.

1 On a hot sunny day cut a square piece from a black garbage bag and stick it to the patio with duct tape. Put a small dollop of honey or jam in the middle of it. Watch and wait. There will be ants walking in a random "drunken" way all over the patio, but eventually one will stumble upon the paradise you have created and it will quickly stuff its little face with a sample and run as fast and as straight as it can back to the nest.

Take it further

* You can have some fun with your ants to demonstrate the total reliance on the scent trail. Watch the path the ants are traveling along and, when you have a gap, quickly smudge the trail with your finger, wiping it backward and forward.

* Watch what happens—when they come to the gap, the ants panic! They scatter and lose their organization. Eventually, in the frantic quest for the trail, one will find it and order will be restored.

Handy stuff: bottle trap

Plastic soda bottles are horrible. Tricky to recycle and around forever, what should we do with them? Well one way to recycle them is to use them to make a "pitfall trap," which is just one lazy way to find out what smaller creatures are roaming around in the weed patch, on the lawn or in the rock garden—especially at night. Follow the steps opposite and then come back the next day to discover what you've caught.

Turn out the contents of your trap into a tub to sort out your catch and to observe the kinds of creatures that were crawling about in your backyard, usually after dark.

Here we have caught a couple of species of ground beetle. These animals are active hunters, running around in the garden eating other insects, and some species even specialize in slug munching. So when you have finished studying them, release your catch and you can let them get on with garden pest control.

2
Put the rotten fruit in the bottom of the main body of the bottle. Smelly meat will attract carnivorous beetles, or dead leaves will attract other types of animal or insect.

3
Invert the top part of the bottle inside the main body.

1
Take your drink bottle and cut around it about 4 inches from the neck. You are left with a "pit" and a funnel. Remove the lid from the funnel.

4
Choose your spot and dig a hole that is the same size and depth as the body of the bottle. Put the bottle in it so that the rim is level with the surface of the soil and then replace the loose soil around the bottle.

5
Place the flat stone, old tile or board over the top so that any passing animals can get underneath but any rain will not fill up the trap, killing any animals that get caught.

Worm world

Most of the time we pay them no attention. They are the pink wiggly things that usually make kids go "yuk!" or adults moan about because they make a mess of the lawn. But there is much more to worms than meets the eye. Not only are they vital to the health of soil, but they are good food for many creatures we love, such as robins and other birds. Worms are also fascinating animals.

You may find them drowning in puddles on pavements on rainy days or uncovered when you are digging. But to see a worm at its best you need to get out after dark and do a little bit of worm watching. Take a flashlight with you and cover it with a thin layer of transparent red cellophane so that you produce a red light the worms will not be sensitive to. Yes—they can see. Worms may not be able to form images like we do, but they are sensitive to light. Shine a flashlight on one without the red covering and you will see what I mean.

The best nights to go worm watching are the warm, wet ones. Walk carefully and slowly around on the grass and you could get to see worms with their front parts out of their burrows. If you are really lucky, you may see worms grabbing dead leaves with their mouths and pulling them back into their burrows to eat.

Next time you find a worm, give it a few seconds of your time. Get to know it a bit better. They don't have ears, but they are nonetheless very sensitive to vibration. Supposing you were to talk to it, which end would you strike up conversation with? Which end is the worm's head? Well, put your worm down and it will be easy enough to work out. The worm's pointed end is where the mouth is and the blunt and flattened tip is the rear of the worm.

Nick's trick

It looks ridiculous, but it is a lot of fun; it's called puddling or worm charming. Gulls do this on wet playing fields. You stamp up and down on the spot while pouring water on the ground at the same time. After a few minutes of this activity, worms should start to come to the surface.

You can tell if your worm is fully grown. If it has a saddle (or clitellum)—a broad band across its middle —you can be sure it's an adult, as young worms do not have one of these.

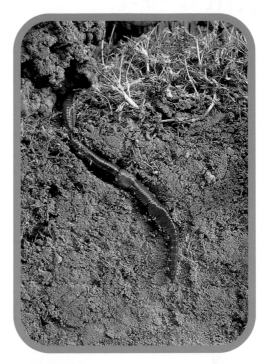

Take it further

* One of the things that is cool about worms is the way they move through the soil. Let one wiggle about on your palm until it finds its way between your fingers —feel how strong it is!

* Feel the motion of the worm—the way it stretches out and becomes thin so it can squeeze between your fingers. It then contracts, squishing the watery body fluids up to the front end, forcing your fingers apart. That is exactly how it moves through the soil.

* To help it grip the tunnel walls, worms also have very strong bristles along their bodies. These are known as setae, and you can feel them if you gently pull a worm backward between your fingers. They feel rough, which is quite surprising for a creature that looks so wet and soft! These setae are also the reason robins have such a hard job pulling worms out of their tunnels on the lawn.

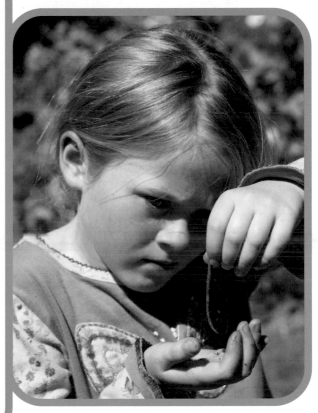

Webbed wonder

It sometimes seems a shame to think that those gorgeous orb webs that you find draped in the shrubbery or hanging in the barn rarely last longer than a day. Being fragile is, of course, part of their attraction, and from the spider's point of view they are designed as disposable and recyclable insect traps. However, it is possible to preserve these structures and even hang them on your own wall.

First of all, choose a nice still day and find a real beauty of a web. Make sure it is dry (no droplets of dew) and make sure its maker, the spider, isn't in residence (check well in and around the edges of the web, especially in curled-up leaves) as it really won't appreciate what comes next! Then follow the steps opposite to make your own lovely spider's web picture.

Fab facts

* Spiders can be found out at sea and in the air, even as high as 6,000 feet. They form part of a strange world of aerial plankton that drift around on air currents. Spiders don't have wings, so how on earth do they get up there?

* Some of them do it by "ballooning." Go out on a dewy fall morning and just about any long grass will be laced with dew-laden strands of silk.

* Investigate closely and you may find lots of tiny "money" spiders. If you collect one on the tip of a finger and hold it up to the breeze or blow on it, you may persuade it to "balloon" for you.

* The spider will raise itself up and the breeze will pull out a thread of silk, which will snake up on the wind. When this develops enough lift to overcome the weight of the spider, it lets go and goes drifting.

> spray paint, white or black is a good choice
> newspaper or large sheet of paper
> artist's fixative (available from art and crafts stores) or hair spray
> **a piece of cardboard large enough for your web to fit onto and contrasting in color to your choice of spray paint**
> scissors

1

Take the can of spray paint and, holding a sheet of newspaper behind the web to stop you getting paint all over the plants, spray the web evenly and lightly on both sides from a distance of about 18 inches. Get too close and you will blow a hole in your web. Leave it to dry for a while and repeat.

2

Spray artist's fixative or hair spray onto the web to make it super-sticky. Repeat on the other side, just as you did with the spray paint.

3

Before the glue dries, take the cardboard and line it up perfectly with the web. Slowly and carefully push the cardboard onto the silk so it sticks in the right place first time. Once the web has touched the cardboard you cannot change your mind without ending up in a messy tangle! Use scissors to cut the supporting strands and give the web and cardboard another coat of fixative to make sure it's securely held in place.

Take it further

Once you've finished your web, mount this spider's original in a frame and hang it on your wall. You could measure all the strands of silk and work out how much silk was needed to make your web, and even collect the webs made by different species of spider.

Going further

This book was never meant to be anything but the very beginning of a journey—I see it as being the map, the compass, and a kick in the right direction. As you continue to various woodland habitats, you will begin to ask more questions and discover things that this book may not be able to answer. This is why this section exists—to give you a few more pointers in the right direction.

Good reading

National Geographic My First Pocket Guide Series (Age 6-10)
> *Backyard Wilderness*
> *Garden Birds*
> *Insects*
> *Reptiles & Amphibians*

National Audubon Society First Field Guides
> *Amphibians*
> *Birds*
> *Insects*
> *Trees*

Peterson Field Guides for Young Naturalists (Age 8-12)
> *Backyard Birds*
> *Butterflies*
> *Caterpillars*
> *Songbirds*
> *Wildflowers*

Stokes Beginner's Guides
> *Birds (Eastern)*
> *Birds (Western)*
> *Bats*
> *Bird Feeding*

> *Butterflies*
> *Hummingbirds*
See also American Birding Association on-line catalog for additional birding books aimed at kids.

Handy organizations

Audubon Societies: There are several tiers of Audubon Societies including the National Audubon Society, which has chapters in many states and large independent Audubon Societies such as Mass Audubon and New Jersey Audubon. Most of these organizations have many programs and sometimes publications for young naturalists.

Defenders of Wildlife: This national conservation organization publishes a well-known magazine for young naturalists called *Ranger Rick*.

Special Interest Clubs: Many states and provinces have clubs devoted to the study of specific taxa: wildflowers, bats, butterflies, etc., and of course birds. These are way too numerous to list here. These clubs are usually glad to have kids come along on field trips. The best way to find these in your area is to go on line and "google" your favorite subject, like "Virginia butterfly club" and see what you get.

Handy stuff - equipment supplies and other contacts

Carolina Biological Supply Company
- www.carolina@carolina.com

Ward's Natural Science
P.O. Box 92912
Rochester, NY 14892-9012
www.wardsci.com

BioQuip Products
2321 Gladwick St.
Rancho Dominguez, CA 90220
www.bioquip.com

The first two are large national companies that have segments specializing in equipment and publications for kids. BioQuip specializes in insect equipment and publications.

Index

Author's acknowledgments

> Big thanks to the energetic and hardworking team at HarperCollins who put this book together. Especially the tireless Helen Brocklehurst—how she holds everything together when it comes to building books, I don't know. But thankfully she does and she's good at it. And the same for Emma Callery, who as editor for this book has endured the frustrating half-finished manuscripts, bad grammar and spelling and, of course, the continual frustration of not being able to get hold of me on the phone! Thanks for not shouting at me and getting cross! Nikki English, the photographer, who has the patience of a saint and found the energy to continue wrangling animals and children both at the same time, AND managing to take great photographs; surely the definition of multi-tasking!

> Sarah Childs-Carlile for the use of her garden and the brilliant models Barney, Billie, Clare, Hattie, Hepsie, Matthew, Solly, and Victoria.
> Chris Leahy at Massachusetts Audubon for invaluable advice on this edition of the book.